CANINE STRESS SIGNALS

SAFETY NOTICE & WAIVER:

Neither the author nor the publisher of this book makes any warranties or guarantees regarding the contents, implications, or results of the contents of this book. Please operate with extreme caution whenever enacting or supervising any and all human-animal interactions or animal-animal interactions. This book is an an introductory text to some of the most basic canine stress signals. We **strongly** recommend consulting with an anti-aversives, certified canine behavior consultant such as a CBCC-KA to learn the intricacies of recognizing canine stress signals and other canine communication and body language. Dog's Heart Press (DHP) and the author expect that anyone obtaining or providing this book to anyone else indemnifies and holds harmless DHP, the author, and all affiliates from all losses, liabilities, damages, costs, or expenses.

Dog's Heart Press
Box 670, Warrenton, OR 97146

Canine Stress Signals
Copyright © 2020 Rain Jordan All Rights Reserved
Cover Image by Carl Barcelo

No part of this book may be reprinted in any form
without the express written permission of the publisher.
For permissions, contact DHP, Box 670, Warrenton, Oregon, 97146.

Printed in the United States of America
ISBN 978-1-935716-49-5

CANINE STRESS SIGNALS
a primer

Rain Jordan

Dog's Heart Press
USA

Contents

Everything Has Its Influence	9
Distress versus Eustress	11
Negative Associations → Negative Emotional States → Undesired Behavior	13
Examples of Canine Distress Signals	15

    In the Ears
    In the Eyes
    In the Face
    In the Head
    In the Body
    In the Legs
    In the Tail
    In Movements and Actions

Closing Thoughts and Resources	29

Everything Has Its Influence

Canine stress has many possible influences, including 1) environment (i.e., any and all situations and stimuli in the dog's world), 2) learning history (e.g., past aversive training and experiences or past positive training and experiences, past development of negative versus positive associations, etc.), 3) health (illness, injury, pain, physical and psycholgical suffering, medications, etc.), 4) breed (genetic/physical differences), and 5) individual differences--which may be argued to be essentially ramifications of the others. What's important to understand here is that we must consider and respect many factors when trying to understand our dogs.

Learning to recognize stress in animal behavior involves understanding contextual variations. Our efforts at recognizing these factors can be greatly helped by taking and analyzing photos, videos, and audio recordings, a thorough examination of the animal's history, and up to date, real time assessments of the animal's current behavior and its antecedents. All of these help us achieve deeper, more complete understanding of our dogs.

The ability to quickly recognize the signals dogs give is an important skill because canine stress signals can provide early information needed to help avoid behavior problems. Therefore, understanding canine stress signals is an important early step in preventing undesired behavior.

Distress versus Eustress

Many things cause stress; even simple and positive changes can cause stress. *Eustress* refers to positive stress, e.g., the excitement of getting ready to go out and play.

It is negative stress--*distress*--we must recognize, avoid, and resolve to help dogs feel safe and to do our part to ensure healthy behavior. Because distress can fuel unhealthy behavior, helping dogs feel safe reduces undesired behavior by reducing distress.

When a dog hides, barks, lunges, or snaps, there's a high likelihood that the recipient of that behavior has done something--however unwittingly--that made the dog feel threatened, thereby building distress in the dog. Dogs can't know a human's intentions and since they don't speak fluent human, they have no way to know who and what are threats to their safety. If your human friend shoves you into a bush as you walk down the street together and you go to punch him in response, he has the luxury of explaining he just saved you from being hit by a car or other oncoming danger, and you have the luxury of understanding, and therefore deciding not to punch him. But instead of understanding and respecting dogs' natural survival behaviors, we sometimes unfairly call dogs "aggressive" for defensive and protective acts taken in response to inefficient human interactions with dogs.

If we say "Come here; I'm not going to hurt you" to dogs

as we push or pull on them, they do not know whether the reason for our behavior is to help or to harm. For all they know, we could be saying, "Get over here so I can eat you." What dogs know, like all of us who have a survival instinct, is that when a threat arises, it should be defended against. What we need to know is how to avoid making dogs feel threatened, how to recognize their signals when they do feel threatened, and how to help them feel safe instead.

Dogs who feel unsafe will be distressed, and distressed dogs are more likely to present with self-defensive behaviors, which humans tend to find undesireable. Self-protective behavior such as running away, hiding, growling, barking, lunging, snapping, or even biting, may be objectionable to us, but to dogs these are part of living; indeed, for dogs, at times they may be the *only* way to keep living. Recognizing the earlier, more subtle signs of canine distress provides people with the possibility of early prevention of undesired behavior and therefore happier lives with dogs.

Negative Associations → Negative Emotional States → Undesired Behavior

When considering examples of canine distress, keep in mind some basic negative states that may be involved:

Fear: Innate emotional response to real or perceived threats.

Anxiety: Anticipation/expectation of future threats even when there is no reason to expect them.

Phobia: An ongoing state of fear that is out of proportion to the actual danger presented by an alarming stimulus.

Arousal: While some arousal is positive (e.g., excitement may be based in feelings of happiness), arousal such as agitation and frustration may be based in feelings of physical or emotional discomfort and may lead to assertion, demand, ritualized aggression (warning behaviors), or actual aggression.

Everything an animal experiences can affect the animal's current and future behavior. This is because associations are created with every new experience, and those associations can then fuel future emotional responses, which can then fuel future behavioral responses. Every new experience that scares or otherwise distresses an animal can thereby create a new negative association with the distressing stimulus, and potentially with any additional stimuli present during that experience. Being able to read dogs' early distress signals, such as those shown in subtle body language, helps us to minimize the development of negative associations and related behaviors.

Examples of Canine Distress Signals

In the Ears

Pinned/Pressed Back

Flattened

In the Eyes

Hard Stare

Squinting or
Repetitious Blinking

Whale Eye

Wide Eye or Dilated Pupils

In the Face

Furrows & Ridges

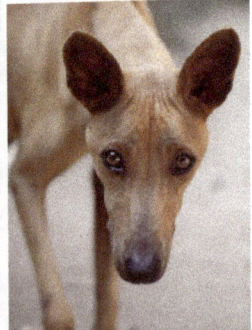

Musculature pulled tight

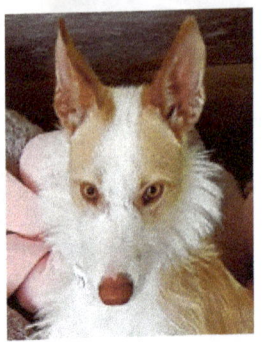

Whiskerbed Puffed

Whiskers Flared, Forward, or Flattened

Wrinkling Muzzle/Nose

Puckered Muzzle

C shape (or short v) Open Mouth

Tightly Closed Mouth
(especially suddenly)

Snarl (open mouth with mainly front
teeth top & bottom showing, OR
one side lip curl, side teeth showing)

Vd corners of stretched back
open mouth

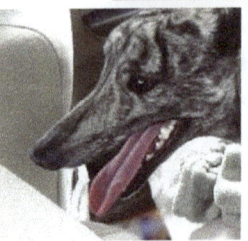

Long Lip Line
(stretched back while closed)

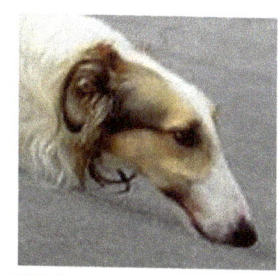

Spatulate Tongue

Lip Lick/
Nose Lick/
Tongue Flick

In the Head

Head Lowered

Head Pressed
into Shoulders

Head Turned Away/Pressed Away

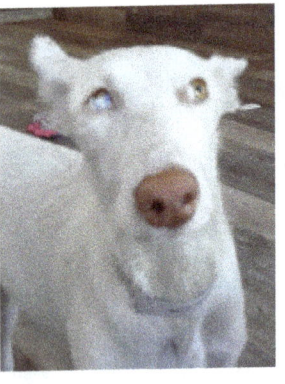

In the Body

Belly Up

Cower/Hunch

Freeze

Increased Shedding

Lean Away

Penile Crowning (no photo)

Piloerection (hackles up)

Straight, Stiffened Back & Legs

In the Legs

Braced

Buckled/Compacted

Conflicted Stance

Paw Lift

Sweating Paw Pads (no photo)

In the Tail

Lowered

Straight Up

Tucked

In Movements and Actions

4 Fs: Fidget (out of context actions e.g., lip lick, sniff, scratch, yawn, etc.), Freeze (stopped movement), Flee (attempt to avoid or escape), Fight (ritualized aggression—intimidative maneuvers designed to scare away threats or perceived threats, or, if these are not heeded, actual aggression, i.e., biting, may follow as a last resort.)

Avoidant: Includes hiding, leaning away, turning away, backing up, rejecting requests to approach or touch, etc.

Escape: Attempts to break out of crates or other confinement, slip out of collar/harness, get away, etc.

Chasing: (dog-dog dynamics) High speed, intensely target focused, without allowing target to escape, rest, or take turn chasing may be or become predatory in nature, either intentionally or as a natural result of increasing excitement from the chase.

Chewing: Excessive chewing, or chewing of non-food items such as fabrics, rocks, self, etc., may imply distress. The same may be true for excessive licking. (Always check with your vet to rule out illness, pain, or compulsive disorder.)

Conflicting Direction: Distress may result in confusion or panic, which may show in legs moving in opposite directions.

example of conflicted movement in the front legs

Growl: If we don't recognize dogs' early distress signals found in their body language, the growl may be a dog's next attempt to communicate "I don't feel comfortable with this situation; please make it stop." Never punish or scold a growl because dogs who are punished for growling are left with snapping and biting as their self-defense options.

Hypersalivation: Excessive drooling

Hypervigilance: Actions suggesting acute high alert. May include pacing forward and back or side to side, spinning, turning head repeatedly (looking for threats), etc.

Lunging: Lunging toward a person, animal, or moving object suggests distress because it is an attempt to move away a real or perceived threat, or because it is an attempt to eliminate perceived competition for a valued resource.

Muzzle Punch: An assertive or self-defensive action of sharply punching a person or other animal with the nose. This is not the same as a playful or soft nose 'boop', which would not typically indicate distress.

Scratching when no itchy stimulus is present.

Shake Off: A whole body shake-off, as if shaking off water, may act as a stress release.

Slow Motion: Often seen in combination with cower or hunch, slow motion movement indicates fear or concern. Stalking also may include slow motion movement, however.

Sharp or Tight Movements: May indicate increased arousal or agitation. If in response to a surprise, especially followed with avoidance/escape motions, the sharp movement may also be an involuntary startle (fear) response.

Shoulder Down: Sometimes seen during dog-dog play and often just before a flop down and belly exposure. May function to de-escalate an unwanted escalation of interaction.

Sniffing: Sniffing areas where no food is or would tend to be. (Some sniffing, however, such as exploration during walks, is positive and provides crucial enrichment for dogs.)

Startle: A sudden response to being surprised. Motions vary but may be a jerking motion, jump, cower, run, hide, brace, compaction, or even a yelp, screech, or bark. Anxious, traumatized, and other fearful dogs may tend to startle easily or have specific startle triggers.

Tremble: Outside of cold temperature contexts, trembling (which is sometimes misinterpreted as cold-response shivering) is a clear indicator of distress.

Sudden Stop or Stiffening of Tail: May suggest feeling suddenly threatened and/or may warn of potential impending assertive action.

Tight Tail Movements: Not all tail 'wags' indicate happiness. A tightly wagging tail may indicate nervousness or rising agitation.

Waving Head: Some dogs may present with rolling waves of the head if aversive control by the collar is attempted.

Yawn: Yawning not associated with sleep, sleepiness, or restful repose may indicate nervousness / distress.

Snarl, Snap, Nip, Bite: Snarls and snaps(aka air snaps) are often attempts to scare away a real or perceived threat. Nips and bites may occur if the threat refuses to retreat, leaving the dog feeling s/he has no other options.

Vocalization: Whining and crying may suggest pain or other physical discomfort, or they may suggest emotional discomfort such as loneliness or unmet needs. Howling may also suggest emotional discomfort or attempt to gain access to comforting, company, or other attention, including of other dogs in the home or area. Barking may indicate fear, alert, alarm, demand, or aggression. Each of these tends to be communicated by a different type of bark, and although there are general rules about this, each dog may be different

Closing Thoughts and Resources

If you notice in your dog any of the distress signals mentioned in this book, please help your dog feel safe rather than threatened. For example, a dog who recoils when a human approaches may need time and space to learn for himself that the human isn't a threat. We can help by behaving in non-threatening ways such as not hovering over or reaching toward the dog but rather giving the dog time, a safe zone, and generous opportunities to choose to approach the human with positive results. Since interpretation of signals can be complex due to contextual variations, I strongly recommend obtaining anti-aversive, professional help to ensure best possible outcomes.

Anti-aversives behavior consultants and trainers can be found on the Fearful Dogs Project website, www.FearfulDogsProject.org, and may also be found on the Certification Council for Professional Dog Trainers site, www.ccpdt.org/dog-owners/certified-dog-trainer-directory.

However, always carefully research and interview trainers, behaviorists and all other service providers to confirm anti-aversives policies before entrusting your pets to them.

More information can be found at ExpertCanine.com, FearfulDogsProject.org, ProtectThemAll.org, and in the books *Such Small Hands: An Anti-Aversives Primer* and *The Dog Who Couldn't Be Petted.*

Acknowledgments

Thanks are owed to the photographers and publishers of the photos in this book, including Shutterstock.com and its artists Agafred, AMFPhotography, Anna Krivitskaya, BaronB, Bildagentur Zoonar GmbH, Bogdan Sonjachnyj, Collette Worley, David P Baileys, EB Adventure Photography, Eric Isselee, FootMade0525, Helioscribe, Kesinee Tong, Martin Dallaire, Masson, Nancy Dressel Photobac, PixieMe, Polina Yurtseva, Susan Schmitz, and Suzi Nelson, and photographers at Unsplash.com.

www.ingramcontent.com/pod-product-compliance
Lightning Source LLC
Chambersburg PA
CBHW061316040426
42444CB00010B/2667